Formal Name: United Mexican States (Estados Unidos Mexicanos).

Short Form: México.

Term for Citizen(s): Mexican(s).

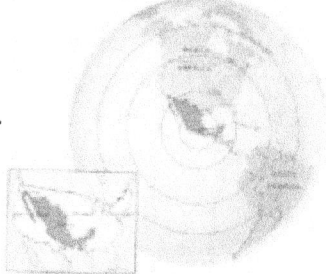
Click to Enlarge Image

Capital: Mexico City (Ciudad de México), located in the Federal District (Distrito Federal) with a population estimated at 8.8 million in 2008.

Major Cities: The Greater Mexico City metropolitan area encompasses Mexico City and several adjacent suburbs, including the populous cities of Ecatepec de Morelos (1.8 million residents in 2005) and Netzahualcóyotl (1.2 million). The total population of the Greater Mexico City metropolitan area is estimated at about 16 million. Other major cities include Guadalajara (1.6 million), Puebla (1.3 million), Ciudad Juárez (1.2 million), Tijuana (1.1 million), and Monterrey (1.1 million).

Independence: September 16, 1810 (from Spain).

Public Holidays: New Year's Day (January 1); Constitution Day (February 5); Birthday of Benito Juárez (March 21); International Labor Day (May 1); Independence Day (September 16); Discovery of America (October 12); Anniversary of the Revolution (November 20); Christmas (December 25); and New Year's Eve (December 31).

Flag: Three equal vertical bands of green (hoist side), white, and red; the coat of arms (an eagle perched on a cactus with a snake in its beak) is centered in the white band.

Click to Enlarge Image

HISTORICAL BACKGROUND

Early Settlement and Pre-Columbian Civilizations: Nomadic paleo-Indian societies are widely believed to have migrated from North America into Mexico as early as 20,000 B.C. Permanent settlements based on intensive farming of native plants such as corn, squash, and beans were established by 1,500 B.C. Between 200 B.C. and A.D. 900, several advanced indigenous societies emerged. During this "Classic Period," urban centers were built at Teotihuacán (in central Mexico), Monte Albán (in the territory now making up the state of Oaxaca), and in the Mayan complexes (in the modern-day states of Chiapas, Tabasco, Campeche, Yucatán, and Quintana Roo, as well as at sites in the modern-day countries of Honduras, Guatemala, and Belize). These advanced societies developed written languages, displayed high levels of occupational specialization and social stratification, and produced elaborate art, architecture, and public works. After the unexplained collapse of the Teotihuacán society around A.D. 650, the early civilizations of central Mexico were eclipsed by the Mayan city-states of the Yucatan Peninsula. The lowland Mayan communities flourished from A.D. 600 to A.D. 900, when they, too, abruptly declined. The Post-Classic period (from about 900 to 1500) was characterized by widespread migration throughout Mesoamerica and the re-emergence of the central valley of Mexico as the site of large-scale urban settlement and political power. By the 1300s, the Aztecs had established themselves on the site of present-day Mexico City. The militaristic and bureaucratic Aztec state ruled a far-flung tributary empire spanning much of Central Mexico.

Spanish Conquest, Colonization, and Christianization: During the early sixteenth century, Spanish military adventurers based in Cuba organized expeditions to the North American mainland. The first major military expedition to Mexico, led by Hernán Cortés, landed near present-day Veracruz in 1519 and advanced inland toward the Aztec capital of Tenochtitlán hoping to conquer central Mexico. By 1521 Spanish forces under Cortés, reinforced by rebellious Indian tribes, had overthrown the Aztec empire and executed the last Aztec king, Cuauhtémoc. The Spanish subsequently grafted their administrative and religious institutions onto the remnants of the Aztec empire. During the early years of colonial rule, the conquistadors and their descendants vied for royal land titles (*encomiendas*) and Indian labor allotments (*repartimientos*). The early colonial economic system was based largely on the ability of the *encomienda* holders (*encomenderos*) to divert Indian labor from agriculture to the mining of precious metals for export to Spain. The *encomienda* became the basis for a semi-autonomous feudal society that was only loosely accountable to the central authorities in Madrid.

New Spain and the Mercantile Economy: During the sixteenth and seventeenth centuries, Mexico experienced far-reaching demographic, cultural, and political change. New Spanish-style cities and towns were founded throughout central Mexico, serving as commercial, administrative, and religious centers that attracted an increasingly Hispanicized and Christianized mestizo population from the countryside. Mexico City, built on the ruins of Tenochtitlán, became the capital of Spain's North American empire. Colonial society was stratified by race and wealth into three main groups: whites (European- and American-born), *castas* (mestizos), and native peoples; each had specific rights or privileges (*fueros*) and obligations in colonial society. New Spain was ruled by a viceroy appointed by the Spanish crown but in practice enjoyed a large degree of autonomy from Madrid.

Throughout the colonial period, Mexico's economic relationship with Spain was based on the philosophy of mercantilism. Mexico was required to supply raw materials to Spain, which would then produce finished goods to be sold at a profit to the colonies. Trade duties that placed stringent restrictions on the colonial economies protected manufacturers and merchants in Spain from outside competition in the colonies. In the mid-eighteenth century, the third Bourbon king of Spain, Charles III, reorganized the political structure of Spain's overseas empire in an effort to bolster central authority, reinvigorate the mercantile economy, and increase tax revenues. New Spain was divided into 12 military departments (*intendencias*) under a single commandant general in Mexico City who was independent of the viceroy and reported directly to the king.

War of Independence: The spread of late eighteenth-century Enlightenment philosophy, together with the egalitarian example of the American and French revolutions, motivated

Mexican-born whites (criollos) to seek greater autonomy and social status within the colonial system. Discrimination against criollos in the granting of high offices had long been a source of contention between Spain and Mexico City. In 1808 the invasion of the Iberian Peninsula by Napoleon Bonaparte and the forced abdication of the Spanish king, Charles IV, disrupted Spain's faltering authority over Mexico. Rejecting the puppet regime installed by France, the incumbent viceroy allied himself with the criollos and declared an independent junta ostensibly loyal to Charles IV. Allies of the Napoleonic regime responded by staging a coup and installing a new viceroy, an action that set the stage for war between criollos and Spanish loyalists.

On September 16, 1810, Miguel Hidalgo y Costilla, a criollo parish priest, issued the Grito de Dolores (Cry of Dolores), a call to arms against Spanish rule that mobilized the Indian and mestizo populations and launched the Mexican war of independence. After a brief siege of Mexico City by insurgents in 1814, Spanish forces waged a successful counteroffensive that had nearly annihilated the rebels by 1820. However, the tide turned in favor of the criollos in February 1821, when a loyalist officer, Augustín de Iturbide, spurned the newly established constitutional monarchy in Spain and defected with his army to the rebels. Under the conservative Plan of Iguala, the rebel army agreed to respect the rights of Spanish-born whites (*peninsulares*) and to preserve the traditional privileges (*fueros*) and land titles of the Roman Catholic Church. The Spanish, now outmaneuvered politically as well as militarily, lost the will to continue the war and recognized Mexican independence in September 1821.

Empire and Early Republic: Upon the withdrawal of Spain, Iturbide declared himself emperor of Mexico and Central America. Within months, however, his imperial regime was bankrupt and had lost the support of the criollo elite. In February 1823, Iturbide was overthrown by republican forces led by General Antonio López de Santa Anna. The Mexican empire was dissolved when the United Provinces of Central America declared their independence in July 1823.

Clashes between the conservative and liberal parties dominated politics during the early republic. Conservatives, who advocated a centralized republic governed from Mexico City and the maintenance of clerical and military *fueros*, had the support of the Roman Catholic Church and much of the army. Liberals, on the other hand, advocated federalism, secularism, and the elimination of *fueros*. Under the federal republic in effect from 1824 to 1836, Mexico was ruled by a series of weak and perennially bankrupt liberal governments. General Santa Anna and his allies fashioned a centralized republic that held power from 1836 to 1855. Although nominally a liberal, Santa Anna was primarily a nationalist who dominated Mexico's politics for two decades. Santa Anna's efforts to assert Mexican government authority over Anglo-American settlements in Texas spurred that region's secession from Mexico in 1835. Excesses committed by a punitive Mexican expedition against Texan garrisons at the Alamo and Goliad provoked strong anti-Mexican sentiment in the United States and galvanized U.S. public support for Texan independence. In April 1836, Texan forces defeated and captured Santa Anna at San Jacinto. During a brief captivity, the Mexican general signed a treaty recognizing Texan independence from Mexico.

Mexican-American War, Civil War, and French Intervention: A dispute with the United States over the boundaries of Texas led to war between the United States and Mexico in April 1846. Two U.S. Army columns advancing southward from Texas quickly captured northern

Mexico, California, and New Mexico, repelling Santa Anna's forces at Buena Vista. An amphibious expeditionary force led by General Winfield Scott captured the Gulf Coast city of Veracruz after a brief siege and naval blockade. Scott's forces subdued Mexico City in September 1847, following a series of pitched battles along the route inland to the Mexican capital and its surrounding bastions. In the ensuing Treaty of Guadalupe Hidalgo, U.S. withdrawal was contingent on Mexico's ceding of the territories of New Mexico and Upper California (the present-day states of California, Nevada, Utah, and parts of Arizona, New Mexico, Colorado, and Wyoming) and its acceptance of the incorporation of Texas into the United States.

In 1855 Santa Anna was ousted and forced into exile by a revolt of liberal army officers. A liberal government under President Ignacio Comonfort oversaw a constitutional convention that drafted the progressive constitution of 1857. The new constitution contained a bill of rights that included habeas corpus protection and religious freedom and mandated the secularization of education and the confiscation of Catholic Church lands. It was strongly opposed by conservatives and church officials who objected to its anticlerical provisions. Seeking to avoid armed conflict, President Comonfort delayed its promulgation and instead decreed his own moderate reform agenda known as the Three Laws. However, in January 1858, after unsuccessful efforts by Comonfort to craft a political compromise, the factions took up arms, and the government was forced from office. A three-year civil war between conservative and liberal armies, known as the War of the Reform, engulfed the country. After initial setbacks, the liberals, led by the prominent Zapotec Indian politician and former vice president Benito Juárez, gained the upper hand. In January 1861, the liberals regained control of Mexico City and elected Juárez president.

In January 1862, the navies of Spain, Britain, and France jointly occupied the Mexican Gulf coast in an attempt to compel the repayment of public debts. Britain and Spain quickly withdrew, but the French remained and, in May 1863, occupied Mexico City. Drawing on the support of the Mexican conservatives, Napoleon III installed Austrian prince Ferdinand Maximilian von Habsburg as Mexican Emperor Maximilian I. By February 1867, a growing liberal insurgency under Juárez and the threat of war with Prussia had compelled France's withdrawal from Mexico. Maximilian was captured and executed by Juárez's forces shortly thereafter. Juárez was restored to the presidency and remained in office until his death in 1872.

Porfirio Díaz Era: From 1876 until 1910, governments controlled by the liberal caudillo Porfirio Díaz pursued economic modernization while maintaining authoritarian political control. In contrast to his liberal predecessors, Díaz established cordial relations with the Catholic Church, an institution he considered central to Mexican national identity. The Díaz years, known as the "Porfiriato" saw heavy state investment in urban public works, railroads, and ports—all of which contributed to sustained, export-led economic growth. The Porfiriato governments encouraged foreign investment in export agriculture and the concentration of arable land in the form of haciendas. Although the urban middle class experienced substantial improvements in quality of life, Mexico's peasant majority found its livelihood threatened by the loss of communal lands to the haciendas. In response to growing unrest in the countryside, Díaz created the Rural Guard, a paramilitary force that became notorious for its repressive tactics.

Mexican Revolution and Aftermath: By the turn of the century, opposition to Díaz had spread among dissident liberals who sought a return to the principles of the constitution of 1857. Following Díaz's fraudulent re-election in 1910, several isolated rural revolts coalesced into a nationwide insurrection. Unable to regain control of several rebellious state capitals, Díaz resigned the presidency in May 1911 and fled to France. A provisional government under the liberal reformer Francisco I. Madero was installed but failed to maintain the support of radical peasants led by Emiliano Zapata, who was conducting a rural insurgency in southern Mexico. Amid general unrest, a counterrevolutionary government under Victoriano Huerta assumed power in February 1913. Huerta's authority was undermined when U.S. Marines occupied Veracruz in response to a minor incident. Following Huerta's resignation in July 1914, fighting continued among rival bands loosely allied with Venustiano Carranza and Francisco "Pancho" Villa. U.S. support for Carranza prompted Villa to retaliate by raiding several U.S. border towns. In response, the United States dispatched troops under General John J. Pershing on an unsuccessful expedition into northern Mexico to either kill or capture Villa. Carranza negotiated a cease-fire among several of the warring Mexican factions in December 1916 and restored order to most of the country by accepting the radical constitution of 1917. Rural violence continued in the south, however, until the assassination of Zapata by Carranza's forces in November 1920. The Mexican Revolution exacted a heavy human and economic toll; more than 1 million deaths were attributed to the violence.

Consolidation of the Revolution: From the 1920s through the 1940s, a series of strong central governments led by former generals of the revolutionary armies governed Mexico. Most Mexican presidents complied with the constitutional provision mandating a single six-year term *(sexenio)* with no re-election. During the late 1920s, President Plutarco Elías Calles established many of the institutions that would define the Mexican political system throughout the twentieth century. This system was based on an authoritarian state controlled by a hegemonic "revolutionary" party headed by a powerful president, economic nationalism, limited land collectivization, military subordination to civilian authority, anticlericalism, and the peaceful resolution of social conflict through corporatist representation of group interests. Tactics such as extensive use of state patronage, manipulation of electoral laws and electoral fraud, government propaganda and restrictions on the press, and intimidation of the opposition helped ensure the decades-long domination of government at all levels by the Institutional Revolutionary Party (Partido Revolucionario Institucional—PRI). Through their top-down control of the PRI, presidents acquired the power to handpick their successors, decree laws, and amend the constitution virtually at will.

The ideology of the revolutionary regime took a leftward turn during the *sexenio* of Lázaro Cárdenas (1934–40). Cárdenas nationalized Mexico's oil industry and vastly expanded the acreage of nontransferable collectivized farms *(ejidos)* set aside for peasant communities. During World War II and the early years of the Cold War, the governments of Miguel Avila Camacho (1940–46) and Miguel Alemán Valdés (1946–52) repaired strained relations with the United States and returned to more conservative policies. In the postwar years, Mexico pursued an economic development strategy of "stabilizing development" that relied on heavy public-sector investment to modernize the national economy. Concurrently, Mexican governments followed conservative policies on interest and exchange rates that helped maintain low rates of inflation and attracted external capital to support industrialization. This dual strategy helped maintain steady economic growth and low rates of inflation through the 1960s.

Crisis and Recovery: During the presidencies of Luis Echeverría (1970–76) and José López Portilllo (1976–82), the public sector grew dramatically, and state-owned enterprises became a mainstay of the national economy. Massive government spending was sustained in part by revenues from the export of newly discovered offshore oil deposits. By the late 1970s, oil and petrochemicals had become the economy's most dynamic sectors. However, the windfall from high world demand for oil would be temporary. In mid-1981, Mexico was beset by falling oil prices, higher world interest rates, rising inflation, a chronically overvalued peso, and a deteriorating balance of payments that spurred massive capital flight. In August 1982, the Mexican government defaulted on scheduled debt repayments—an event that heralded a regionwide debt crisis. President López Portillo responded to the crisis by nationalizing the banking industry, further undermining investor confidence. His successor, Miguel de la Madrid Hurtado (1982–88), implemented economic austerity measures that laid the groundwork for economic recovery. In September 1985, the country suffered another blow when two major earthquakes struck central Mexico. Between 5,000 and 10,000 people are believed to have died and 300,000 left homeless in the worst natural disaster in Mexico's modern history. Many victims lost their lives in modern high-rise buildings constructed in violation of safety codes. The high death toll and the government's inadequate response to the disaster further undermined public confidence in the PRI-dominated political system.

In the run-up to the 1988 presidential and congressional elections, a splinter faction of left-wing former PRI members opposed to market reforms rallied behind the independent presidential candidacy of Cuahtemoc Cárdenas. In the first competitive presidential election in decades, the PRI candidate, Carlos Salinas de Gortari, was declared the winner with a bare majority of the vote. Numerous irregularities in the vote tally, including an unexplained shutdown of the electoral commission's computer system, led to widespread charges of fraud. Overcoming a weak mandate and strong opposition from organized labor, President Salinas undertook a sweeping liberalization of the economy. Reforms included the privatization of hundreds of state-owned enterprises, liberalization of foreign investment laws, deregulation of the financial services sector, and across-the-board reductions in tariffs and nontariff trade barriers. Economic liberalization culminated in the negotiation of the North American Free Trade Agreement (NAFTA) with Canada and the United States in 1992. Salinas's reforms were overshadowed by subsequent revelations of corruption within the top echelons of the PRI, as well as by the unexpected emergence of a rural insurgency in the southern state of Chiapas.

Despite the assassination of the original PRI candidate, Luis Donaldo Colosio, the presidential election proceeded as scheduled in the fall of 1994. The replacement PRI candidate, Ernesto Zedillo Ponce de León, managed to stave off a serious challenge from the center-right National Action Party (Partido de Acción Nacional—PAN) to win the presidency.

Transition to Democracy: During the mid-1990s, an economic crisis stemming from an unsustainable current account deficit and mismanagement of the government bond market plunged Mexico into a severe recession. President Zedillo spent much of his *sexenio* restoring macroeconomic balance and responding to demands for greater accountability and transparency of public institutions. Zedillo also had to contend with the Zapatista rebellion in Chiapas, which highlighted the poverty and marginalization that characterized many of Mexico's indigenous communities. In the political realm, the Zedillo administration advanced electoral system reforms that leveled the playing field for opposition parties and set the stage for a genuine transition to democracy. The July 1997 midterm elections left the PRI with a minority of seats in the Chamber of Deputies (the lower house of Congress), expanded opposition control of state governorships, and gave the left-wing Party of the Democratic Revolution (Partido de la Revolución Democrática—PRD) control of Mexico City's government.

The opposition's momentum carried over into the September 2000 general elections. The PAN candidate, Vicente Fox Quesada, won the historic presidential race, becoming the first opposition head of state since the consolidation of the revolution. President Fox promised a deepening of Mexico's economic and political reforms, declared "war" on organized crime, and planned to negotiate an immigrant "guest worker" program with the United States. Despite strong public support early in its term, the Fox administration was weakened by the PAN's loss of congressional seats during the 2003 midterm elections and the government's failure to craft a legislative coalition in support of its reform agenda. By the end of his term in 2006, much of President Fox's structural reform program remained unfulfilled.

On July 2, 2006, Mexico held general elections for president, all seats in Congress, and several state governorships. The presidential race was closely contested between the PAN candidate, former Fox administration energy minister Felipe Calderón Hinojosa, and the PRD candidate, populist former mayor of Mexico City Andrés Manuel López Obrador. The PRI candidate, former Tabasco governor Roberto Madrazo Pintado, trailed in the race, as voters appeared wary of returning the PRI to the presidency. Opinion polls indicated that the election was largely a referendum on Mexico's two decades of market-oriented economic reforms. Calderón promised to continue the reform agenda by promoting greater foreign investment and increasing the competitiveness of Mexico's economy through structural reforms of the pension and labor laws. He also pledged to continue the government's fight against the drug cartels and to improve public safety. By contrast, López Obrador vowed to focus on Mexico's domestic problems, such as poverty and social inequality, and to halt so-called "neo-liberal" reforms. He promised to create thousands of jobs by funding massive public works projects and affirmed that he would seek to renegotiate NAFTA in order to protect Mexican farmers from an influx of imported U.S. corn. Further, López Obrador vowed to break up the unpopular commercial oligopolies that emerged from the privatization of state assets during the 1990s.

Official tallies showed the results of the presidential election to be extremely close. Initial uncertainty about the accuracy of the preliminary vote count led both of the leading candidates to claim victory. However, subsequent official tabulations by the independent Federal Electoral Institute (Instituto Federal Electoral—IFE) confirmed that Calderón had indeed won the election by a slim plurality of 35.89 percent versus López Obrador's 35.31 percent of the vote (a margin of victory of 244,000 votes out of 41.8 million cast).

The results of the 2006 congressional races saw both the PAN and the PRD gain seats at the expense of the formerly dominant PRI. For the first time in its history, the PRI lost its plurality of seats in both houses of Congress, an event observers interpreted as a further sign of the party's decline. Nonetheless, the PRI retained a sufficiently large bloc of seats to remain an influential congressional force and was well positioned to become a coalition partner of any future Mexican government. The PRD retained control of the powerful mayoralty of Mexico City. All three major parties held state governorships.

During 2007, the Calderón administration made public safety and the fight against drug cartels its highest domestic priorities. In response to escalating drug violence, the federal government deployed 24,000 troops to various states and removed hundreds of corrupt police officials. Mexican public opinion strongly backed Calderón's aggressive tactics against the drug gangs. Under Calderón's leadership, the center-right PAN government courted the center-left PRI in an effort to advance the president's legislative agenda. During the 2007 legislative session, Congress passed far-reaching fiscal and pension system reforms that had stalled during the Fox administration.

By mid-2008 successive Mexican governments had made progress in reforming the economy and reducing extreme poverty. However, significant disparities in wealth, high levels of crime, and corruption persisted. The less-developed states in the south continued to lag economically behind the more prosperous north and center, fueling illegal migration to the United States. Mexico's economy was also lagging behind those of other middle-income countries, such as China, in terms of overall competitiveness. In addition to further consolidating Mexico's transition to democracy, the 2006 general elections presented an opportunity to overcome executive-legislative stalemate and move toward consensus on economic and public-sector reforms.

GEOGRAPHY

Click to Enlarge Image

Location: Mexico is located in the southern portion of North America, bordering the southwestern United States from California to Texas. The southernmost Mexican states of Quintana Roo, Campeche, and Chiapas define the northern border of the isthmus of Central America.

Size: Mexico has an area of 1,964,375 square kilometers—making it the third largest nation in Latin America (after Brazil and Argentina).

Land Boundaries: Mexico has 4,301 kilometers of international land borders: 3,152 kilometers with the United States, 956 kilometers with Guatemala, and 193 kilometers with Belize.

Disputed Territory: Mexico has no outstanding international territorial disputes.

Length of Coastline: Mexico has a 10,143-kilometer coastline: 7,338 kilometers on the Pacific Ocean and Gulf of California and 2,805 kilometers on the Gulf of Mexico and Caribbean Sea.

Maritime Claims: Mexico claims a territorial sea of 12 nautical miles, a contiguous zone of 24 nautical miles, an exclusive economic zone that extends 200 nautical miles off each coast and covers approximately 2.7 million square kilometers, and a continental shelf of 200 nautical miles or to the edge of the continental margin.

Topography: Mexico has a varied topography consisting mainly of plateaus in the eastern two-thirds of the national territory and a mountainous spine running through the western third of the country. The interior north of the Mexico City metropolitan area is mainly high plateau—known as the Mesa Central and Mesa del Norte. The average elevation in the plateaus ranges from about 900 meters in the north to 2,400 meters in the southern portion of the Mesa Central. In the far northwest, the Baja Peninsula stretches southeast from the U.S. border for 1,300 kilometers. The peninsula is extremely dry and rugged, with a very narrow coastal plain. The southern highlands, located south of the Mesa Central, contain a number of steep mountain ranges, deep valleys, and dry plateaus. The Yucatan Peninsula extends northeast from the Isthmus of Tehuantepec into the Gulf of Mexico. It is a flat, low-lying limestone plateau lacking in major rivers. Mexico has several massive mountain ranges, most of which extend from northwest to southeast: the Sierra Madre Occidental in the west, the Sierra Madre Oriental in the east, and the Sierra Madre del Sur in the south. Lesser ranges include the Sierra Madre de Chiapas and the Cordillera Neovolcánica—an east-to-west volcanic range spanning the breadth of the country just south of Mexico City. The country's highest point, the Pico de Orizaba (5,636 meters), is located within the Cordillera Neovolcánica about 193 kilometers southeast of Mexico City. Mexico has extensive lowlands largely along the Gulf coast and in the Yucatan Peninsula.

Principal Rivers: Mexico has nearly 150 rivers, two-thirds of which empty into the Pacific Ocean and the remainder into the Gulf of Mexico or the Caribbean Sea. Most rivers are short and non-navigable, running from coastal mountain ranges to the coast. Water volume is unevenly distributed throughout the country. Five rivers—the Usumacinta, Grijalva, Papaloapán, Coatzacoalcos, and Pánuco—account for 52 percent of the average annual surface water volume. Most of the larger rivers are located in the southeastern part of the country and flow into the Gulf of Mexico. Northern Mexico contains less than 10 percent of the country's water resources. The Río Bravo del Norte (known as the Rio Grande in the United States) defines Mexico's northern border from Ciudad Juárez east to the Gulf of Mexico.

Climate: Mexico experiences great climatic variation owing to its considerable north-south extension and variations in elevation. The climate of much of northern and central Mexico is characterized by high temperatures and moderate to low rainfall. The highlands of the central plateau generally have a moderate climate with few extremes of hot or cold. Temperatures in Mexico City, for example, range from an average of 17° C in July to 12° C in January. The northern and central areas of the plateau are arid to semiarid; the drier regions receive about 300 millimeters of rainfall annually. Annual rainfall increases to about 600 millimeters in the southern part of the plateau, including the Mexico City area. The northern coastal areas, including Baja California, are arid. Rainfall along the Pacific Coast averages just 130 millimeters, as compared with 250 to 600 millimeters along the northern Gulf coast. Much of southern Mexico has a tropical climate with distinct rainy and dry seasons. Temperatures in the coastal regions range from 21° C to 27° C. Annual rainfall, which ranges from 1,500 millimeters to 2,000 millimeters, occurs mainly during the rainy season of May to October. The Gulf coast is subject to hurricanes.

Natural Resources: Mexico has abundant natural resources. In addition to extensive subsoil resources (including large reserves of oil and silver), the country has a rich biodiversity and varied wildlife. As of 2003, about 5 percent of Mexico's land area was under a protected status. Protected sites included six wetlands of international importance (Ramsar sites) totaling 1.1 million hectares and 12 biosphere reserves totaling 6.8 million hectares.

Land Use: Although nearly half of Mexico's total land area is officially classified as agricultural, only 12 percent of the total area is cultivated. Extensive irrigation projects carried out in the 1940s and 1950s greatly expanded Mexico's cropland, especially in the north. One-third of Mexican territory is officially designated as grazing land. These lands are located mainly in the north. Some 9 percent of Mexico's territory consists of forest or woodland, 59 percent of which is in the tropics, 15 percent in the subtropical zone, and 26 percent in the temperate and cool zones. Temperate forests cover some 49 million hectares, almost one-third of which are open to logging, mainly in the states of Chihuahua, Durango, and Michoacán.

Environmental Factors: Mexico faces significant environmental challenges affecting almost every section of the country. Vast expanses of tropical and subtropical forests in the south have been denuded for cattle raising and agriculture. Deforestation has contributed to serious levels of soil erosion nationwide. Soil destruction is particularly pronounced in the north and northwest. More than 60 percent of land is considered in a total or accelerated state of erosion. The result is a mounting problem of desertification throughout the region. Mexico's coastline is threatened by inadequately protected petroleum extraction in the Gulf of Mexico, which has damaged marine ecosystems. Mexico City is one of the world's most polluted urban areas. Vehicle emissions and other airborne contaminants have been blamed for a wide range of respiratory illnesses. Polluted water from Mexico City has been linked to congenital birth defects and high levels of gastrointestinal illnesses in the neighboring state of Hidalgo. Government antipollution measures have met with limited success.

Time Zones: Most of Mexico, including Mexico City, is in the Central Time zone (Coordinated Universal Time (UTC)/Greenwich Mean Time (GMT) –6 hours). The state of Northern Baja California is on Pacific Time (UTC/GMT –8 hours). The states of Baja California Sur, Sonora, Sinaloa, Chihuahua, and Nayarit are on Mountain Time (UTC/GMT –7 hours). In Mexico, however, Mountain Time is usually referred to as "Pacific Time" because most of these states border the Pacific Ocean. The state of Quintana Roo is on Eastern Time (UTC/GMT –5 hours). Mexico uses daylight saving time (DST). During 2008 DST was scheduled for April 6 to October 26.

SOCIETY

Population: In mid-2008 Mexico had an estimated population of 106.7 million. The population growth rate has been falling since the 1970s, declining from an average of 3.4 percent annually during the 1960s to 1.8 percent annually in the 1990s. The decrease is largely attributable to declining fertility. Emigration to the United States has increased significantly since the 1970s. The number of Mexican-born residents in the United States grew from an estimated 760,000 in 1970 to 8.5 million in 2000 (8.7 percent of Mexico's population in the 2000 census).

Immigration has not been a significant factor in population growth since the 1920s. Nationwide, population density was 52 residents per square kilometer according to the 2000 census. Density varied widely among the 31 states and Federal District from a high of 5,975 residents per square kilometer in the Federal District to a low of 12 residents per square kilometer in Baja California Sur. Mexico experienced heavy urbanization during the latter half of the twentieth century. In 1950 less than half the population (42.6 percent) lived in communities of 2,500 or more inhabitants. By 2005 more than three-quarters (76.2 percent) of Mexicans lived in such communities. The national population is heavily concentrated in central Mexico along a roughly northwest to southeast axis from Guadalajara to Veracruz. This area includes the heavily populated contiguous states of Jalisco, Guanajuato, Michoacán, Hidalgo, México, Distrito Federal, Morelos, Puebla, and Veracruz–Llave—which together are home to about half the national population. Major urban agglomerations are also found in the north, centered on the cities of Ciudad Juárez, Tijuana, and Monterrey—with more than 1 million residents each. In the south, the largely Amerindian populations in the states of Chiapas and Oaxaca live mainly in small- to medium-sized towns and villages.

Demography: Mexico's birthrate has been declining since the 1960s. During the 1990s, the rate of natural increase was 1.6 percent, half the rate observed during the 1960s (3.1 percent). In 2008 there were an estimated 20.0 live births and 4.8 deaths per 1,000 population. Life expectancy at birth was estimated at 75.8 years overall (73.1 years for men and 78.8 years for women). The total fertility rate (children born per woman) was 2.4. Infant mortality stood at 19.0 per 1,000 live births in 2008, compared to 79.3 deaths per 1,000 live births in 1970. The 2008 age structure of the population was as follows: 0–14 years, 30 percent; 15–29 years, 27 percent; 30–49 years, 27 percent; 50–64 years, 10 percent; 65 years and older, 6 percent. The median age was 26 years, and females slightly outnumbered males by a ratio of 1.04:1. As a result of declining fertility and rising life expectancy, by 2025 Mexico's population is predicted to age overall; the share of the youngest cohort (0–14) will decline to 24 percent, and that of the oldest will rise to 10 percent.

Ethnic Groups: The two main ethnic categories of mestizo and Indian/Amerindian are defined broadly along cultural rather than racial lines. The term "mestizo" describes persons with a solely European background, those with a mixed European–indigenous ancestry, and indigenous people who have adopted the dominant Hispanic societal values. According to anthropologists, the terms "Indian" or "indigenous" describe persons who identify themselves as such, use an indigenous language in daily speech, remain actively involved in indigenous communal affairs, or participate in religious ceremonies rooted in native American traditions. Approximately 60 percent of the population is mestizo, 30 percent Amerindian or predominantly Amerindian, 9 percent white or European, and 1 percent "other."

Languages: Spanish is the dominant language for both the mestizo and Indian populations. Approximately 6 million Mexicans spoke an indigenous language as a first language in 2000. The number of indigenous language speakers rose slightly in absolute terms from 1990 to 2000 but declined slightly as a percentage of the total Mexican population (7.2 percent in 2000 versus 7.8 percent in 1990). Indigenous speakers are highly concentrated in the southern states of Guerrero, Oaxaca, Quintana Roo, Chiapas, and Yucatán. Among indigenous language speakers, 83 percent also speak Spanish, while about 1 million are monolingual. Linguistically isolated communities are most prevalent in the states of Chiapas and Guerrero. Specialists have identified

12 distinct Mexican indigenous linguistic families, more than 40 subgroups, and at least 90 individual languages. According to the 2000 census, nearly 24 percent of all native speakers spoke Náhuatl, the language of the Aztec people and the most geographically dispersed native language. Other major indigenous languages include Maya, Zapotec, Mixtec, Otomí, Tzeltal, and Tzotzil.

Religion: Roman Catholicism is the main religion; 88 percent of the population five years of age and older identified themselves as Roman Catholic in the 2000 census. Protestants and Evangelicals were the second largest religious group, accounting for approximately 5 percent of the population. The rapid growth in Protestant and Evangelical membership slowed during the 1990s, averaging a 3.7 percent annual rise from 1990 to 2000 (versus 10 percent during the 1970s and 5 percent during the 1980s).

Education and Literacy: During the past several decades, Mexico has made significant advances in literacy and the provision of public education. In 2004 the adult literacy rate stood at 91 percent (92 percent among men and 90 percent among women). Mexican law mandates universal preschool, primary, and secondary education. Eleven years of education are compulsory, but in practice the average number of years of schooling for the population 15 and over was around eight years during 2005. That year, Mexico had 27.1 million students in primary, secondary, and postsecondary educational institutions. Enrollment rates in primary education are high (97 percent of girls and 98 percent of boys); however, many students—especially those from poor families—do not complete high school, opting instead to enter the workforce. Seventy percent of eligible students were enrolled in secondary education in 2006. Education accounts for a quarter of public spending—the highest share of public spending on education among Organisation for Economic Co-operation and Development (OECD) countries. Notwithstanding the proportionally large education budget, spending per student is low by international standards—about a quarter of the OECD average for primary education and a third of the OECD average for secondary education. Most current spending at the primary and secondary levels goes to the compensation of staff, leaving few resources for infrastructure, supplies, and training. The performance of Mexican secondary school students in math, reading, and science is the lowest of all OECD countries and ranks well below the OECD average.

Health: Aggregate health statistics have improved greatly since the 1970s. However, Mexico lags well behind other OECD countries in health status and health care availability. Total health care spending accounted for 6.4 percent of gross domestic product (GDP) in 2005; per capita spending on health care was US$675 (adjusted for purchasing power parity)—about a quarter of the OECD average. During 2005, 45.5 percent of health spending was paid from public sources—comparable to the share of public spending in the United States but significantly below the OECD average. Private financing in Mexico is almost entirely in the form of out-of-pocket payments, as only 3.1 percent of total expenditures on health are funded through private health insurance. In 2005 Mexico had 1.8 doctors and 2.2 nurses per 1,000 population, a significant increase in health care personnel over the previous decade but again below the OECD averages for these indicators. The mortality rate for children younger than five years was 27 per 1,000 live births in 2005. Ninety-seven percent of the population had direct access to potable water and 79 percent to sanitation. In 2005 the incidence of human immunodeficiency virus/acquired immune deficiency syndrome (HIV/AIDS) among persons aged 15 to 49 was 0.3 percent.

Welfare: Mexico has made progress in reducing poverty since the late 1990s, performing above the Latin American average. However, nearly half the population continues to live in poverty; about 15 percent of the total population subsists in extreme poverty, with limited access to food and basic services. Residents of southern Mexico consistently trail the rest of the country in quality-of-life indicators. Urban workers in the informal sector of the economy do not have access to the same level of health care as their counterparts in the formal sector, nor do they qualify for retirement or pension benefits. About half the workforce is registered with the Mexican Social Security Institute.

ECONOMY

Overview: Mexico is a middle-income country with a developing market economy that is closely linked to the much larger economy of the United States. Mexico's economy ranks as "moderately free" in the *2008 Index of Economic Freedom* (a joint publication of the *Wall Street Journal* and the Heritage Foundation). From the 1940s through the late 1960s, successive governments followed an economic strategy of import substitution and fiscal and monetary restraint intended to promote growth while holding inflation in check. During the 1970s, populist governments abandoned fiscal discipline and oversaw a massive expansion of consumer subsidies and state ownership of productive sectors. Unsustainable public-sector spending backed by over-reliance on oil export revenues and abundant international credit contributed to chronically high inflation and wild fluctuations in economic performance. As a result, the economy experienced spurts of rapid growth followed by sharp recessions in 1976 and 1982. The mid- to late 1980s were years of economic austerity and stagnant growth during which Mexico was able to balance its national accounts while combating high inflation. Gross domestic product (GDP) grew at an average rate of just 0.1 percent per year between 1983 and 1988. During these years, monetary policy was severely restricted and public-sector spending sharply curtailed.

The late 1980s and early 1990s saw far-reaching market-oriented structural reforms, including privatization of hundreds of state-owned enterprises, liberalization of foreign investment laws, deregulation of the financial services sector, and across-the-board reductions in tariffs and nontariff trade barriers. These reforms, which culminated in the ratification of the North American Free Trade Agreement (NAFTA) in 1994, attracted an influx of US$148 billion in foreign direct investment (FDI) during the next decade. From 1988 to 1994, GDP growth averaged 2.6 percent annually, sustained by exports and an influx of foreign capital. However, the collapse of the peso in December 1994 and the ensuing economic crisis erased most of the real wage gains from the previous years. In response to the 1994 crisis, Mexico passed legislation granting greater independence to its central bank. Growth resumed in the late 1990s, but the recovery was cut short by the spillover effects of the 2001 recession in the United States. Since 2002, a worldwide commodity price boom, a U.S. economic recovery, and sound macroeconomic policies have helped boost economic growth while allowing inflation to remain in the single digits.

The economy is hampered by structural weaknesses that limit Mexico's potential for future growth and job creation. Mexico's workers are generally low skilled and have less schooling than workers in advanced industrial economies. This deficit in human capital manifests itself in stagnant labor productivity and real wages, as well through the existence of a large "informal" labor sector that deprives the education, health care, and social security systems of crucial tax revenues. Income distribution remains highly unequal; about half of Mexico's population lives in poverty.

Despite recent reforms, some public policies continue to hold back the economy's competitiveness and growth potential: rigid labor and commercial codes discourage hiring and inhibit informal workers from transitioning into the formal economy; the important energy sector, which remains state-owned, suffers from numerous inefficiencies and undercapitalization; and the federal government relies heavily on the oil industry for revenues, which consequently renders public budgets vulnerable to cyclical fluctuations in hydrocarbon prices. Whereas the liberalizing reforms associated with NAFTA have been a boon to northern and central Mexico's manufacturing centers, few new jobs have materialized for the predominantly agricultural states in the south and southwest. This uneven development pattern has failed to slow large-scale wage migration to the United States. As global competition for capital investment has increased— particularly from low-cost manufacturing in Asia—Mexico's status as a premier export hub for the North American market has eroded.

Gross Domestic Product (GDP): Nominal GDP stood at US$879.2 billion dollars in 2007 (US$1.23 trillion in terms of purchasing power parity, or PPP), representing a per capita GDP of approximately US$8,088 (US$11,337 in terms of PPP)—the highest in Latin America. In 2008 Mexico was entering its fifth consecutive year of economic expansion. Annualized real GDP growth slowed from of a peak rate of 4.8 percent in 2006 to 3 percent in 2007, partly as a result of a slowdown in the U.S. economy. Economic output in 2007 was divided among the sectors as follows: services, 70 percent; industry, 26 percent; and agriculture, 4 percent.

Government Budget and Public Finance: During 2007, Mexico's public-sector budget was balanced, with expenditures matching revenues of US$209 billion (equivalent to 24 percent of gross domestic product). The public sector typically relies on profits from the state-owned hydrocarbons sector for a quarter of its revenues. Federal tax revenue is derived from several sources: corporate and individual income taxes, a nationwide value-added tax, and excise taxes on the mining industry. State and local governments rely heavily on federal government revenue transfers for their budgets.

Inflation: Inflation has trended generally downward since the late 1980s (when it exceeded 150 percent), thanks to a commitment by successive governments and the independent central bank to anti-inflationary fiscal and monetary policies. During 2007, annual inflation was approximately 4 percent.

Agriculture, Forestry, and Fishing: In 2007 agriculture accounted for only 4 percent of gross domestic product but employed 18 percent of the labor force. Agricultural practices range from traditional techniques, such as slash-and-burn cultivation of indigenous plants for family subsistence, to the use of advanced technology and marketing in large-scale, capital-intensive export agriculture. The staple food crops are maize, wheat, sorghum, barley, rice, beans, and potatoes. The principal cash crops are coffee, cotton, sugarcane, fruit, and vegetables. Other important agricultural goods include beef, poultry, dairy products, and wood products.

Agricultural exports, valued at US$7 billion in 2006, are destined primarily for the United States. Forestry production is geared toward the exploitation of domestic fuelwood, sawlogs for construction, and pulpwood for processing in domestic paper mills. Mexico's coastal fishing grounds offer a rich variety of fish and other seafood. The Pacific coast accounts for nearly three-quarters of Mexico's total catch, producing mainly lobster, shrimp, croaker, albacore, skipjack, and anchovies. Mexico's Gulf and Caribbean waters produce shrimp, jewfish, croaker, snapper, mackerel, snook, and mullet. In 2005 the total catch exceeded 1.4 million metric tons.

Non-fuel Mining and Minerals: Mexico has abundant mineral resources and is the world's second-largest producer of silver. During 2007 silver production was approximately 2.3 million metric tons. Other significant mining products in 2007 were iron (7.3 million metric tons), sulphur (1.0 million metric tons), fluorite (0.92 million tons), zinc (0.42 million metric tons), copper (0.32 million metric tons), and manganese (0.16 million metric tons). Mexico also possesses substantial deposits of mercury, bismuth, antimony, cadmium, phosphates, and uranium.

Industry and Manufacturing: Manufacturing is the economy's leading export sector, accounting for 81 percent of total export revenues in 2007 and about a quarter of gross domestic product. About a quarter of Mexico's labor force is engaged in some type of industrial or manufacturing activity. The manufacturing sector was transformed by the liberalizing reforms of the late 1980s and early 1990s, which privatized hundreds of state enterprises and greatly expanded opportunities for foreign direct and portfolio investment. Manufacturing attracts about half of all foreign direct investment in Mexico, two-thirds of which is concentrated in the *maquiladora* sector, comprising more than 2,000 businesses employing 1.13 million workers in 2004. Overall manufacturing output is dominated by three activities: machinery and equipment (primarily the automotive sector); food, beverages, and tobacco; and chemicals, petrochemicals, rubber, and plastics. Together, these three sectors account for three-quarters of manufacturing output. Other components of manufacturing output include textiles, clothing, and leather goods; metals; and paper products. Principal industrial centers are located in and around the Mexico City metropolitan area, Monterrey, and Guadalajara.

Energy: The state oil corporation, Petróleos de Mexico (Pemex), holds a constitutionally established monopoly on the exploration, production, transportation, and marketing of the nation's oil and natural gas. In 2006 Mexico was the sixth-largest producer of oil in the world, and the second largest in the Western Hemisphere. About half of Mexico's crude oil production is consumed domestically, while the other half is exported—mainly to the United States. The country extracted an average of 3.1 million barrels per day of crude oil in 2007. Over the past two decades, the oil sector's share of total export revenues has fallen sharply as the economy has diversified and as an increasing share of production has been dedicated to meeting domestic demand. Crude oil exports accounted for 15.6 percent of total export revenues in 2006 versus 61 percent in 1985. Mexico's proven oil reserves have declined substantially since 2000, from 26.9 billion barrels to less than half that amount by 2007. Barring new oil discoveries, Mexico is expected to curtail its oil exports within the next few years.

In addition to crude oil, Mexico had 434 billion cubic meters of proven natural gas reserves in 2006. Since the late 1980s, Mexican demand for natural gas has outpaced production. As a result, Mexico imported 9.7 billion cubic meters of natural gas in 2005, representing about one-fifth of national consumption. Pemex retains sole control of natural gas exploration and production and operates an extensive pipeline network consisting of approximately 453 pipelines spanning 4,700 kilometers.

Mexico has 1.3 billion tons of recoverable coal reserves. During 2006 it produced 13 million short tons of coal while consuming 21 million short tons. Most coal consumption is for electricity generation, while the remainder is for steelmaking.

Mexico has a single nuclear power plant. The 1,400-megawatt Laguna Verde plant is located near Veracruz.

Mexico generated 240 billion kilowatt-hours of electric power in 2006: 79 percent from conventional thermal sources, 13 percent from hydroelectricity, 4 percent from nuclear power, and 3 percent from geothermal, wind, or solar energy. The bulk of conventional thermal capacity in the national electricity grid consumes fuel oil, followed by coal and natural gas. Electricity demand is projected to grow by 6 percent per year during the next decade.

Services: Services (including financial services) make up the largest segment of the Mexican economy, accounting for 70 percent of gross domestic product (GDP) in 2007 and employing about 60 percent of the national workforce. In recent years, major transnational retailers have expanded their presence in the country. Merchandise counterfeiting and intellectual property rights crimes are pervasive within the informal retail sector, threatening the profitability of the formal retail sector. Tourism, which caters primarily to U.S. and Canadian travelers, accounts for about 1 percent of GDP.

Banking and Finance: Financial services represent the most advanced component of the services sector, accounting for about a quarter of all foreign investment. In 2006 more than 80 percent of banking sector assets were foreign-owned. Mexico has a central bank (Banco de México) and six types of banking institutions: public development banks, public credit institutions, private commercial banks, private investment banks, savings and loans associations, and mortgage banks. Other components of the financial system include securities market institutions, development trust funds, insurance companies, credit unions, factoring companies, mutual funds, and bonded warehouses. Since 1994, Banco de México has been largely autonomous. The bank is governed by a five-member board composed of a chairperson or "governor" and four "subdirectors." The governor serves a six-year term; subdirectors serve eight-year terms and are appointed on a staggered basis. All members are appointed by the president but once confirmed may not be removed except in cases of gross misconduct or incapacitation as outlined in the Central Bank Law.

Labor: In 2006 the labor force was estimated at 44.5 million (out of a total population of 107 million). Approximately 1 million new workers enter the labor force annually; however, the Mexican economy typically creates only about half as many new jobs. The Mexican labor market is characterized by the existence of an informal sector, in which workers are mostly unskilled, do not pay taxes, and do not receive benefits, and a formal sector, in which jobs generally require more skills, and working conditions and benefits are regulated by strict labor

16

laws. The informal sector is estimated to make up between 40 and 65 percent of the total labor force. During 2007 Mexico reported a low unemployment rate of approximately 4 percent; however, real wages have stagnated during the past decade, and 25 percent of the workforce is believed to be underemployed. In 2007 the labor force was distributed by occupation as follows: services, about 60 percent; industry, about 25 percent; and agriculture, about 18 percent.

Foreign Economic Relations: Mexico's extensive trade linkages to the United States dominate its foreign economic relations. In 2006 the leading markets for Mexican products in terms of percentage of total exports were the United States, 84.7 percent; Canada, 2.1 percent; Germany, 1.3 percent; and Spain, 1.2 percent. Mexico's leading suppliers in terms of percentage of total imports were the United States, 50.9 percent; China, 9.5 percent; Japan, 5.9 percent; and South Korea, 4.2 percent. Since the early 1990s, Mexico's foreign economic relations have emphasized active participation in the World Trade Organization (WTO) and the negotiation of free-trade agreements (FTAs)—most notably the North American Free Trade Agreement (NAFTA) with Canada and the United States. Mexico has entered into regional and bilateral FTAs involving more than 40 countries.

Trade Balance: Since the late 1990s, the overall merchandise trade balance has been slightly negative, largely as a result of growing deficits with the European Union and Asia (mainly China). During 2007 Mexico's total merchandise imports were valued at US$280.1 billion versus US$269.1 billion in exports. Mexico's trade deficit with the rest of the world is largely offset by a trade surplus with the United States. This surplus has grown steadily since the late 1990s, driven initially by the boom in manufacturing exports and, more recently, by high world oil prices. In 2006 Mexico's trade surplus with the United States stood at US$81.4 billion.

Balance of Payments: In recent years, Mexico has overcome a historical pattern of unsustainable high current account deficits. Since the late 1990s, the current account deficit has shrunk to sustainable levels of generally less than 3 percent of gross domestic product (GDP). Current transfers—made up largely of wage remittances from Mexicans living in the United States—have become an important contributor to Mexico's external accounts, providing capital inflows estimated to be as much as 2.5 percent of GDP. In 2006 Mexico's current account deficit was estimated at US$1.7 billion.

External Debt: Total external debt was US$165 billion in 2006. At 19 percent of gross domestic product (GDP), Mexico's external debt-to-GDP ratio is one of the lowest in Latin America. The debt-service ratio (the ratio of debt service to export earnings) has declined from 25.5 percent in 2001 to an estimated 15.8 percent in 2005.

Foreign Investment: Mexico is the largest host of foreign direct investment (FDI) in Latin America. During 2006 the stock of FDI in Mexico was US$236.2 billion. During the 10-year period following the ratification of the North American Free Trade Agreement (1994–2004), Mexico attracted a cumulative US$148 billion in FDI, about 50 percent of which was invested in manufacturing and another 25 percent directed toward the financial services sector. Net portfolio investment has been rising since 2002; by mid-2005, foreign holdings of government bonds totaled approximately US$10 billion, while foreign investment in the Mexican stock market exceeded US$85 billion.

Foreign Aid: The World Bank is the leading provider of foreign expertise and financial support to Mexico. Presently, the bank is financing 32 projects in the country, with an average annual commitment of up to US$1.7 billion. The World Bank's 2005–2008 Country Assistance Strategy (CAS) for Mexico projects loans totaling about US$4.8 billion during the strategy's four-year timeline and is designed to support the government's commitment to fighting poverty and inequality.

Currency and Exchange Rate: Mexico's currency is the peso (MXN). In early July 2008, the exchange rate was approximately US$1=MXN10.

Fiscal Year: Calendar year.

TRANSPORTATION AND TELECOMMUNICATIONS

Overview: Mexico's economy relies heavily on the country's road network and maritime ports for the transportation of cargo. The extensive road system handles the bulk of domestic passenger and cargo surface transportation, while airports are struggling to keep up with the growth in international passenger travel. In recent years, the privatization of railroads and ports and the granting of toll road concessions have attracted substantial foreign investment and encouraged modernization of facilities.

Roads: Mexico has one of the most extensive road networks in Latin America, linking nearly all areas of the national territory. In 2005 the country had 235,670 kilometers of roads, 122,677 kilometers of which were paved. The network includes 6,336 kilometers of modern toll highways. Although extensive, much of Mexico's public road system is in poor condition as a result of insufficient investment in maintenance and an overreliance on heavy trucks to haul overland cargo. Roads handle 59 percent of total cargo transportation and 99 percent of domestic passenger journeys.

Railroads: Railroads transport 10 percent of total cargo and play only a minor role in passenger travel. The rail system consists of 26,662 kilometers of track, nearly all of which is made up of 1.435-meter, standard-gauge line. The largest rail line historically has been the state-owned Mexican National Railways (Ferrocarriles Nacionales Mexicanos—FNM), which owns about 70 percent of total track. During the late 1990s, the FNM was broken up into regional rail lines and privatized. The newly privatized entities were granted 50-year leases to operate on the rail system's main routes. By 2004, 81 percent of total rail traffic was handled by private companies. Mexico City maintains a subway system comprising eight lines with 135 stations and a total route length of 158 kilometers.

Ports: The maritime port system has grown rapidly from about 75 ports in the mid-1990s to 108 ports in 2008 with the expansion of international trade. The system has experienced an influx of foreign capital as a result of the comprehensive privatization of port facilities begun during the 1990s. The largest ports, located on the Pacific coast, include Manzanillo, Lázaro Cárdenas, Salina Cruz, Guaymas, and Mazatlán. Important ports on the Gulf Coast include Veracruz,

Tampico, and Coatzacoalcos. During 2007 Mexican ports handled 240 million tons of cargo (mostly petroleum and derivatives, followed by bulk mineral and agricultural products). Container ports moved about 2.7 million twenty-foot equivalent units (TEUs) in 2006. Cruise ship passenger arrivals nearly tripled from 2.3 million in 1997 to 6.4 million in 2007, corresponding to 3,082 cruise ship arrivals in 2007.

Inland Waterways: Mexico's 2,900 kilometers of navigable rivers and coastal canals play only a minor role in the transportation system.

Civil Aviation and Airports: Mexico's civil aviation system is extensive and includes 227 airports—35 of which are international airports—and approximately 1,800 airfields and airstrips nationwide. During 2006 Mexican airports handled approximately 45.4 million passenger journeys, 29.0 million of which were conducted on domestic airlines and 16.4 million on international airlines. The busiest airports are Mexico City (Benito Juárez—MEX), Guadalajara (Miguel Hidalgo y Costilla—GDL), Monterrey (General Mariano Escobedo—MTY), and Cancún (CUN). Despite recent capital expenditures on terminals and runways, the largest airports are struggling to meet rising demand for air transportation services.

Telecommunications: Since the 1990s, telecommunications services have been transformed by privatization of the national telephone company and the advent of wireless technologies. Following the privatization of Teléfonos de México (Telmex) and the opening of the sector to other private carriers in the 1990s, fixed-line density rose from 6.4 lines per 100 in 1990 to 18 lines per 100 in 2006. The latter figure corresponds to approximately 20 million fixed telephone lines in use. Availability of residential fixed-line service varies greatly by region; Mexico City and the more developed northern states experience much higher service densities than the eight poorest southern states. The continued high cost of fixed-line services, together with an incomplete build-out of the fixed-line network, has contributed to a proliferation of mobile telephone use. The number of mobile cellular telephone accounts rose from 14 million in 2000 to more than 57 million in 2006. That year, approximately 22 million Mexicans were classified as Internet users. Major telecommunications infrastructure includes 120 domestic satellite earth stations, 52 international stations, and an extensive microwave radio relay network.

GOVERNMENT AND POLITICS

Political System: Mexico is a federal republic consisting of 31 states and a Federal District. During much of the twentieth century, Mexico was ruled by authoritarian governments under the control of the Institutional Revolutionary Party (Partido Revolucionaro Institucional—PRI). The PRI exercised hegemony over the political system while observing formal democratic procedures, such as regular elections, tolerance of opposition parties, and political campaigning. Mexico's political system historically has concentrated power in the executive branch. By exercising strong leadership over the PRI party apparatus as well as their extensive constitutional prerogatives, Mexican presidents wielded formidable influence over public policy. Since 1997, however, when the first opposition-controlled Congress in Mexico's modern history was voted into office, a more balanced relationship among the branches has developed. Following a series of political and electoral system reforms, the PRI lost its seven-decade monopoly on the presidency in the 2000 elections. The development of a three-party system at the national level has led to a more even distribution of power and has given rise to coalition-style politics. Mexican federalism has historically been weak. State and local governments rely heavily on the federal government for revenues.

Constitution: Mexico's formal government institutions are defined by the constitution of 1917, which is widely regarded as an expression of popular will that guarantees labor and civil rights, electoral democracy, and national independence. Inspired by both socialist and classical liberal political philosophy, as well as by earlier Mexican constitutions, the drafters prescribed a federal republic with separation of powers, recognized a broad range of political and social rights, and treated many matters of public policy explicitly. Key provisions include Article 27, which, before being amended in 1992, imposed stringent restrictions on the ownership of property by foreigners and the Catholic Church and declared national ownership of the country's natural resources; and Article 123, which affirms a variety of labor rights, including the right to organize and an eight-hour workday, and provides for the protection of women and minors in the workplace. Constitutional amendments may be passed with a two-thirds vote of both chambers of the federal Congress and ratification by a majority of the state legislatures. The constitution has been amended extensively since 1917. Major amendments include the granting of women's suffrage in 1953, the easing of nationalist restrictions on foreign investment in 1992, and numerous electoral system reforms during the 1980s and 1990s.

Branches of Government: The federal executive branch is headed by the president and 18 cabinet-level ministers (secretaries). The president holds the formal titles of chief of state, head of government, and commander in chief of the armed forces. Presidents are elected directly by a simple majority of registered voters in the 31 states and the Federal District. Presidents serve a six-year term (*sexenio*) with no possibility of re-election; there is no vice president. If the presidential office falls vacant during the first two years of a *sexenio*, the Congress designates an interim president, who, in turn, must call a special presidential election to complete the term. If the vacancy occurs during the latter four years of a *sexenio*, the Congress designates a provisional president for the remainder of the term. The president has sole authority to appoint and dismiss cabinet secretaries—except for the attorney general, who must receive the consent of the Senate.

The bicameral Congress is composed of a Senate and a Chamber of Deputies. The Senate's 128 seats are filled by a mixture of direct election and proportional representation (96 by direct election and 32 by proportional representation from party lists). In the lower chamber, 300 deputies are directly elected to represent single-member districts, and 200 are selected by a modified form of proportional representation from five electoral regions. Senators are elected to six-year terms, and deputies serve three-year terms. All members of Congress are barred from immediate re-election but may serve nonconsecutive terms. The powers of Congress include the right to pass laws, impose taxes, declare war, approve the national budget, approve or reject treaties and conventions made with foreign countries, and ratify diplomatic appointments. The Senate addresses all matters concerning foreign policy, approves international agreements, and confirms presidential appointments. The Chamber of Deputies oversees all matters pertaining to the government's budget and public expenditures. Each legislative chamber has a number of committees that study and recommend bills. If there is disagreement between the chambers, a joint committee is appointed to draft a compromise version.

The judicial branch is divided into federal and state systems. Additionally, justice of the peace courts are available at the municipal level. Federal district courts exercise broad jurisdiction over federal crimes and writ of injunction (*amparo*) suits and civil controversies regarding the enforcement or application of federal laws or international treaties, among others. The rulings of federal district courts may be reviewed by collegiate and unitary circuit courts and by the Supreme Court. The federal judicial system is organized into 29 circuits, encompassing 172 collegiate circuit courts, 62 unitary circuit courts, and 285 district courts. The Supreme Court is made up of 11 justices (including the chief justice). The court holds biennial sessions in which it is divided into two chambers: Civil and Criminal Affairs and Administrative and Labor Affairs.

Supreme Court justices are appointed by a two-thirds vote of the Senate from among a list of candidates submitted by the president. In the event that two-thirds of the Senate cannot agree on an appointee, the president may fill the vacancy without Senate approval. Justices serve a single 15-year term without the possibility of reappointment. The chief justice is elected from among the sitting justices by a collegial vote of the membership. He or she presides over the court for a term of four years. Chief justices may not serve consecutive terms but may be reelected by their colleagues during their 15-year tenure on the court. District and circuit judges are appointed by the Federal Judicial Council, a quasi-independent judicial branch agency chaired by the chief justice of the Supreme Court. The seven-member council is in charge of carrying out judicial career laws, overseeing judicial functioning, and selecting judges at all levels below the Supreme Court. In addition to the chairmanship, three seats are occupied by judges appointed by the Supreme Court, two seats by notable judicial scholars appointed by the Senate, and one seat by a presidential appointee. Except for the chief justice, all council members serve a single five-year term.

Administrative Divisions: Mexico is a federal republic with 31 states and a Federal District encompassing Mexico City and its immediate environs. Approximately 2,000 municipalities are legally recognized.

State and Local Government: Each of Mexico's 31 states has its own constitution modeled on the national charter and has the right to legislate and levy taxes other than interstate customs duties. Following the federal organization at the national level, state and local governments also have executive, legislative, and judicial branches. The state executive branch is headed by a governor, who is directly elected for a six-year term and may not be reelected. State legislatures are unicameral, consisting of a single Chamber of Deputies that meets in two ordinary sessions per year, with extended periods and extraordinary sessions when needed. Deputies serve three-year terms and may not be immediately reelected. Legislative bills may be introduced by the deputies, the state governor, the state Superior Court of Justice, or a municipality within a given state. Governors appoint the justices of the Superior Court of Justice with the approval of state legislatures. These magistrates, in turn, appoint all lower state court judges. Municipal governments, headed by a mayor or municipal president (*regente*) and a municipal council (*ayuntamiento*), are popularly elected for three-year terms.

Judicial and Legal System: Mexico's judicial system is largely derived from Spanish and Napoleonic civil and criminal codes. The most powerful juridical instrument is the writ of *amparo* (literally, "refuge"), a writ of injunction that can be invoked against acts by any government official. The trial system consists of a series of fact-gathering hearings during which the court receives documentary evidence or testimony, after which a judge in chambers reviews the case file and issues a final written ruling. The record of the proceeding is not available to the general public; only the parties involved have access to the official file and then only by special motion. The law provides for the right of the accused to attend the hearings and to challenge the evidence or testimony presented. The law also guarantees the right to an attorney, although in actual practice the understaffed public defender system is characterized by low professional standards, and, as a result, most indigent defendants are inadequately represented.

In June 2008, the president signed into law legislation reforming the federal legal system to introduce public, oral trials and guaranteeing to defendants the presumption of innocence. Following its passage by both legislative chambers, a constitutional amendment was approved by a majority of Mexico's 31 state legislatures. (Approval by 17 state legislatures is required for the amendment to become law.) Implementation of the reform is to be completed by 2016.

Electoral System: Article 41 of the constitution of 1917 and subsequent amendments regulate electoral politics in Mexico. Suffrage is universal for all citizens 18 or older, and voting is compulsory, although this provision is rarely enforced. The constitution enshrines the principle of direct election by popular vote of the president and most other elected officials. Executive officeholders may not be reelected, and legislators may not serve consecutive terms. Ordinary elections are held every six years for the president and members of the Senate and every three years for deputies. Gubernatorial elections are distributed throughout a six-year presidential term (*sexenio*), so that no more than six governorships are contested in any given year. Elections at the federal, state, and local levels are administered by the Federal Electoral Institute (Instituto Federal Electoral—IFE). The IFE is a semi-autonomous organization established by the 1990 electoral code, consisting of representatives from government and the major political parties. During the 1990s, reforms of the IFE strengthened its capacity to serve as a nonpartisan electoral commission. These reforms included the introduction of majority nonpartisan representation (six out of 11 seats) on the IFE governing board, a legal framework for Mexican and foreign observers to monitor elections, and an independent audit of the national voter list. Voting procedures and requirements incorporate numerous safeguards against fraud, including mandatory voter registration cards bearing photo identification and fingerprints. An autonomous, seven-member Electoral Tribunal adjudicates election disputes.

Politics and Political Parties The Institutional Revolutionary Party (Partido Revolucionario Institucional—PRI) was the country's preeminent political organization from 1929 until the early 1990s. Historically, the PRI has been ideologically a center-left party, blending nationalism with mildly redistributionist public policies. Since its founding, the PRI has portrayed itself as a champion of workers and landless peasants. However, during the mid-1980s the "technocratic" wing of the party, which favored market-oriented reform, became dominant over its populist wing. Over the course of three general election cycles (1982, 1988, and 1994), the PRI's leadership selected presidential candidates primarily based on their ability to implement market-oriented reforms. This trend alienated much of the PRI's populist "*político*" wing, prompting many party members to defect to organizations farther to the left.

Until the early 1980s, the PRI's position in the Mexican political system was hegemonic, and opposition parties posed little or no threat to its power base or its near monopoly of public office. This situation changed during the mid-1980s as opposition parties of the left and right began to seriously challenge PRI candidates for local, state, and national offices. On the right, the National Action Party (Partido de Acción Nacional—PAN) has made the greatest inroads into national politics—most notably by attaining the presidency in 2000 and ending seven decades of PRI control over the executive branch. The PAN emerged as a conservative reaction to the nationalizations and land confiscations undertaken by PRI governments in the 1930s. Its power base is heavily concentrated in the wealthier states of the north and center of the country. The PAN resembles a standard Christian Democratic party, deriving its early support primarily from the Roman Catholic Church, the business sector, and other groups alienated by the left-wing populist policies of past PRI governments. On the left, the Democratic Revolutionary Party (Partido Revolucionario Democrático—PRD) emphasizes social welfare concerns and opposes most economic reforms implemented since the mid-1980s. Although it encompasses much of the rank and file of the former communist and socialist parties, the PRD is controlled by former PRI leaders. Several minor parties also are represented in the Congress and in state and local governments: the Labor Party (Partido del Trabajo—PT), Mexican Green Ecologist Party (Partido Verde Ecologista Mexicano—PVEM), New Alliance Party (Partido Nueva Alianza), and Social Democratic and Rural Alternative Party (Partido Democracia Social y Alternativa Rural).

Mass Media: Mexico is considered the media capital of Spanish-speaking Latin America. The country has approximately 300 daily newspapers, 1,300 radio stations, and 460 television stations, most under private ownership. Television is the most influential medium; a majority of stations are affiliated with either the Televisa or Tele Azteca national networks. The press is largely free; however, liberal defamation and libel laws have been widely cited as a constraint on press freedoms. Violence against journalists by drug smuggling gangs poses a growing threat to freedom of expression, especially in northern Mexico.

Foreign Relations: Historically, Mexico has sought to advance its interests abroad and to project its influence largely through moral persuasion. In particular, Mexico has been a champion of the principles of nonintervention and self-determination. However, during the administration of President Vicente Fox Quesada (2000–2006), Mexico took a more active stance on Western Hemisphere regional issues such as trade promotion, economic development in Central America, migration, combating organized crime, and human rights. Mexican foreign policy has also shifted away from economic nationalism to embrace globalization and participation in international commerce. During its first year, the Felipe Calderón Hinojosa administration (2006–) signaled that it would retreat somewhat from its predecessor's activist approach to international affairs, while continuing to promote domestic economic and political reforms.

The bilateral relationship with the United States is at the forefront of Mexican foreign policy. Since 1981, the management of the broad array of U.S.–Mexico issues has been formalized in the U.S.–Mexico Binational Commission, composed of numerous U.S. cabinet members and their Mexican counterparts. The commission holds annual plenary meetings, and many subgroups meet during the course of the year. The most important U.S.–Mexico bilateral issues are illegal immigration, drug trafficking and border crime, and the promotion of trade and investment. Mexico has urged the United States to enact an expanded guest worker program that would increase opportunities for legal migration of Mexican nationals. Mexico also advocates the granting of amnesty to Mexican illegal immigrants already in the United States and opposes the deployment of fencing across the U.S.–Mexico border. Since the early 1990s, Mexico and the United States have collaborated closely in combating the illegal drug trade.

Membership in International Organizations: Mexico is a member of numerous international organizations, including the following: Agency for the Prohibition of Nuclear Weapons in Latin America and the Caribbean (OPANAL), Asia Pacific Economic Cooperation (APEC) forum, Bank for International Settlements (BIS), Caribbean Development Bank (CDB), Central American Bank for Economic Integration (BCIE), Council of Europe (CE) (observer), European Bank for Reconstruction and Development (EBRD), Food and Agriculture Organization (FAO), Group of Three (Colombia, Mexico, Venezuela—G–3), Group of Six (G–6), Group of Fifteen (G–15), Group of Twenty-four (G–24), Inter-American Development Bank (IADB), International Atomic Energy Agency (IAEA), International Bank for Reconstruction and Development (IBRD), International Civil Aviation Administration (ICAO), International Confederation of Free Trade Unions (ICFTU), International Criminal Court (ICC), International Criminal Police Organization (Interpol), International Development Association (IDA), International Federation of Red Cross and Red Crescent Societies (IFRCS), International Finance Corporation (IFC), International Fund for Agricultural development (IFAD), International Hydrographic Organization (IHO), International Labor Organization (ILO), International Maritime Organization (IMO), International Monetary Fund (IMF), International Olympic Committee (IOC), International Organization for Migration (IOM), International Organization for Standardization (ISO), International Red Cross Movement (ICRM), International Telecommunication Union (ITU), Inter-Parliamentary Union (IPU), Latin American Economic System (LAES), Latin American Integration Association (LAIA), North American Free Trade Agreement (NAFTA), Non-Aligned Movement (NAM) (observer), Nuclear Energy Agency (NEA), Organisation for Economic Co-operation and Development (OECD), Organization for the Prohibition of Chemical Weapons (OPCW), Organization of American States (OAS), Permanent Court of Arbitration (PCA), Rio Group (RG), United Nations (UN), United Nations Conference on Trade and Development (UNCTAD), United Nations Educational, Scientific and Cultural Organization (UNESCO), United Nations High Commissioner for Refugees (UNHCR) executive committee, United Nations Industrial Development Organization (UNIDO), United Nations Institute for Training and Research (UNITAR), United Nations Monitoring, Verification, and Inspection Commission (UNMOVIC), Universal Postal Union (UPU), World Confederation of Labor (WCL), World Customs Organization (WCO), World Federation of Trade Unions (WFTU), World Health Organization (WHO), World Intellectual Property Organization (WIPO), World Meteorological Organization (WMO), World Tourism Organization (WToO), and World Trade Organization (WTO).

Major International Treaties: Mexico is a party to numerous arms control, commercial, and environmental treaties, as well as several regional and bilateral free-trade agreements: Act of Chapultepec, Basel Convention on the Trans-boundary Movement of Hazardous Wastes,

Biological Weapons Convention, Chemical Weapons Convention, Convention on Biological Diversity, Convention on International Trade in Endangered Species, Convention on the International Maritime Organization, Convention to Combat Desertification, Framework Convention on Climate Change (UNFCCC), General Agreement on Tariffs and Trade (GATT), Geneva Protocol, Hague Conventions, Inter-American Democratic Charter, Kyoto Protocol to the UNFCCC, Law of the Sea Treaty, Limited Test Ban Treaty, Mexico–Bolivia Free Trade Agreement (FTA), Mexico–Chile FTA, Mexico–Colombia–Venezuela (Group of Three) FTA, Mexico–Costa Rica FTA, Mexico–European Union FTA, Mexico–Israel FTA, Mexico–Nicaragua FTA, Mexico–Northern Triangle (Guatemala, El Salvador, Honduras) FTA, North American Agreement on Environmental Cooperation, North American Free Trade Agreement (NAFTA), Nuclear Non-Proliferation Treaty (NPT), Renunciation of War Treaty, Rio Declaration on Environment and Development, Terrorism Prevention Convention, Treaty for the Prohibition of Nuclear Weapons in Latin America (Treaty of Tlatelolco), United Nations Conference on Disarmament, United Nations Convention on the Law of the Sea, Rome Statute of the International Criminal Court, Vienna Convention for the Protection of the Ozone Layer, and World Trade Organization (WTO) Agreement.

NATIONAL SECURITY

Armed Forces Overview: Mexico maintains one of the smallest militaries in the Western Hemisphere in per-capita terms. In 2007 Mexico had 237,800 active armed forces personnel and 39,899 reservists. Active-duty personnel are assigned to the various services as follows: army, 183,700; navy, 42,400 (including 12,600 marines); and air force, 11,700. The armed forces' primary missions are domestic antidrug operations, rural counterinsurgency, and disaster relief.

Foreign Military Relations: Historically, relations between the military establishments of Mexico and the United States have not been close. Cooperation peaked for a brief period during and after World War II. In the Cold War atmosphere that followed, however, Mexico opposed U.S. concepts of regional security. During the late 1980s, relations between the Mexican and U.S. military establishments improved as cooperative efforts expanded in the fight against illicit drugs. Numerous Mexican officers receive training in the United States and are well acquainted with U.S. military doctrine, but on the whole, the Mexican armed forces are less influenced by the U.S. military than are the armed forces of other countries in Latin America.

External Threat: Mexico has no foreign nation-state adversaries and little ambition to impose itself upon other nations. It repudiates the use of force to settle disputes and rejects interference by one nation in the affairs of another. Although it has not suffered a major terrorist incident, Mexico considers itself a potential target for international terrorism.

Defense Budget: In 2007 Mexico's defense budget was US$3.3 billion or about 0.4 percent of gross domestic product.

Major Military Units: The principal units of the Mexican army are nine infantry brigades and a number of independent regiments and infantry battalions. The main maneuver elements of the army are organized in three corps, each consisting of three infantry brigades, all based in and around the Federal District. Distinct from the brigade formations, independent regiments and battalions are assigned to zonal garrisons (45 in total) in each of the country's 12 military regions. Infantry battalions, composed of approximately 300 troops, generally are deployed in each zone, and certain zones are assigned an additional motorized cavalry regiment or an artillery regiment. The air force is organized into two wings and 10 air groups, as well as an airborne brigade. The air force's principal base is located at Santa Lucía in the state of México. Other major air bases are located in the states of Baja California Sur, Oaxaca, Quintana Roo, Veracruz, and Yucatán. The navy's operational command is divided between the nation's two coasts. The Pacific fleet is headquartered at Acapulco; the Gulf of Mexico coast command is located at Veracruz. Each command has three naval regions. There are 17 naval zones, one for each coastal state; some are subdivided into sectors. In addition to the surface fleet, the navy maintains an aviation arm and a marine force.

Major Military Equipment: The army is equipped with 272 reconnaissance vehicles, approximately 757 armored personnel carriers, 114 towed artillery, six self-propelled artillery, 1,955 mortars, 30 antitank guns, eight antitank guided weapons, 80 air defense guns, and an unspecified number of surface-to-air missiles. The navy inventory includes one destroyer, six frigates, 180 patrol and coastal combatants, three amphibious landing ships, and 19 logistics and support vessels. Naval aviation maintains 150 unarmed helicopters and eight combat aircraft. The navy's marine component is equipped with 16 towed howitzers, six multiple rocket launchers, 100 mortars, 25 assault amphibious vehicles, and 60 coastal assault craft. The air force has 84 combat aircraft and 123 helicopters.

Military Service: The navy and air force are all-volunteer services, while the 183,700-strong army includes 60,000 conscripts. Army conscripts are selected by lottery and are obligated to serve for one year. All male natural-born Mexican citizens are required to register for the selective service in January of the year in which they reach 18 years of age.

Paramilitary Forces: The Federal Preventive Police (Policía Federal Preventiva—PFP) under the Public Security Secretariat (Secretaría de Seguridad Pública—SSP) combats organized crime and domestic insurgencies. The PFP, which relies heavily on reassigned military police and intelligence personnel, includes several specialized tactical and investigative elements, an independent intelligence arm, the federal highway police, a border and port security branch, and an internal affairs component. In 2007 Mexico had 30,700 paramilitary forces, of which 12,700 were PFP and 18,000, Rural Defense Militia.

Foreign Military Forces: None present.

Military Forces Abroad: Consistent with its foreign policy of non-intervention in the affairs of other states, Mexico has declined United Nations (UN) requests for peacekeeping troops. However, in 2004 the Mexican Foreign Ministry stated that Mexico would be willing to contribute non-combat personnel to UN peacekeeping missions. Mexico has dispatched unarmed troops to Central America and Indonesia to provide humanitarian relief in the aftermath of major natural disasters. In September 2005, a Mexican army convoy delivered humanitarian supplies to survivors of Hurricane Katrina in Texas. Mexico maintains military attachés in several friendly foreign capitals.

Police: Police forces number aproximately 500,000 federal, state, and municipal officers. The paramilitary Federal Preventive Police (Policía Federal Preventiva—PFP) is the main enforcement arm of the federal government. The Federal Investigation Agency (Agencia Federal de Investigación—AFI) under the Office of the Attorney General is a multiskilled investigative agency comparable to the U.S. Federal Bureau of Investigation (FBI). The Special Unit Against Organized Crime (Unidad Especializada Contra la Delicuencia Organizada—UEDO), an investigative arm of the Office of the Attorney General, was specially created to combat organized crime.

Internal Threat: Mexico faces numerous internal threats to public safety, most notably from established domestic drug trafficking networks that transport and distribute South American cocaine and other illicit substances destined for the United States. The country's heavily armed, territorially organized drug trafficking networks regularly launch sophisticated, lethal attacks on police, rival drug gangs, journalists, and elected officials. During 2007 President Calderón committed his government to dismantling the country's narcotics trafficking cartels and mobilized more than 20,000 army troops and federal police against drug traffickers in 10 states. According to media reports, drug cartels killed approximately 2,470 persons, including 300 police officers and 27 soldiers, during 2007. Violence against police officials was particularly severe in the states of Monterrey, Guerrero, Michoacan, and Sinaloa. Street crime and targeted crimes such as kidnapping for ransom are common in major cities. Demonstrations and labor disputes occasionally turn violent. In 2006 the city of Oaxaca experienced a prolonged series of civil disturbances that resulted in approximately 20 civilian deaths. Politically inspired domestic insurgencies pose a minor, but persistent threat to public safety, mainly in the remote, mountainous zones of western and southern Mexico.

Terrorism: Several violent left-wing guerrilla groups have been active in Mexico since the late 1960s. These groups engage in kidnappings for ransom as well as sporadic terrorist attacks against police, military personnel, and the nation's economic infrastructure. Mexico's government officially recognizes the existence of three insurgent organizations. The best known is the Zapatista National Liberation Army (Ejército Zapatista de Liberación Nacional—EZLN), with which the government has had an uneasy truce since the insurgents staged a violent, short-lived 1994 revolt in the southern state of Chiapas. The other two are the People's Revolutionary Army (Ejército Popular Revolucionario—EPR), which operates mainly in Guerrero and Oaxaca states, and an EPR offshoot formed in 1998 called the Revolutionary Army of the Insurgent People (Ejército Revolucionario del Pueblo Insurgente—ERPI). In July 2007, the EPR bombed a major gas pipeline from Mexico City to Guadalajara in western Mexico, causing the temporary shutdown of several foreign-owned factories. The EPR struck again in September, when it bombed six oil and gas pipelines in the state of Veracruz.

Mexico's drug trafficking gangs have begun to use improvised explosive devices (IEDs) and high-powered military-grade weapons in their attacks against rival gangs and police personnel. In February 2008, drug traffickers were suspected of setting off an IED near Mexico City's police headquarters in an attack that killed one person and wounded two others.

Mexico historically has been a haven for Latin American and Spanish militant groups, including the Basque Fatherland and Liberty (ETA) and Revolutionary Armed Forces of Colombia

(FARC) terrorist organizations. Increased intelligence and law enforcement cooperation between Mexico and the governments of Colombia and Spain in recent years has helped reduce the presence of these groups in Mexico. Given its status as a major U.S. commercial partner and ally against terrorism, Mexico considers itself a potential target for attacks by the al Qaeda terrorist network. Since the 2001 terrorist attacks on the United States, Mexico has upgraded border security and deployed its armed forces at critical infrastructure sites throughout the country.

Human Rights: According to the U.S. Department of State, during 2007 the government of Mexico generally respected and promoted human rights at the national level; however, violations persisted at the state and local levels. Government efforts to improve respect for human rights were offset by a deeply entrenched culture of impunity and corruption, particularly among elements of the law enforcement community. As in much of Latin America, prison conditions generally are poor. The law prohibits discrimination based on race, gender, disability, or religion. Although the government continued to make progress in enforcing these provisions, significant problems, particularly violence against women, persisted. There was a marked increase during the year in narcotics trafficking-related violence, especially in the northern border region.